(inner work)ing
Copyright © 2026 Rowan Lay

Front Cover and Interior Art by Connor Davis

The font used is Aptos Display
The cover font is Sylfaen Regular

Gnashing Teeth Publishing
242 East Main Street
Norman AR 71960
http://GnashingTeethPublishing.com

Printed in the United States of America

ISBN 978-1-966075-11-0

Gnashing Teeth Publishing First Edition

(inner work)ing

rowan stuart lay

foreword

Thank you for taking a moment of your life to open yourself to poetry and thank you for taking a moment of your life to listen to art that for me has led to personal growth and transformation.

This has been both years in the making as well as a promising opportunity for future expansion with gratitude and love, and I could not be more excited to share this debut collection and to share my journey.

This collection draws heavily from my lived experiences learning to thrive beyond struggles with chronic mental illness, substance abuse, and suicide attempts, and there are times where this collection is very emotionally raw. Please read gently if your heart is also heavy.

Thank you for taking this journey with me, I will see you on the other side with love.

rowan

for you, the fighter, for you, the dreamer
there is work to be done
and
there is progress to be celebrated

table of contents

preparing in stillness

today
i have shown up to the page
i have prepared a place
should the magic, itself, uncage

this is my sanctuary
this is my stage

may all who visit here
experience the spirit
of my authentic soul
come free of its chains

darkness

the bathtub of my chest keeps leaking

i think that if i write words
powerful enough to spin the world
i will have written words
large enough to fill the hole in my soul

and so i write

as though it was ever meant to be filled

i fear i come in too many pieces (some assembly required)

the problem with wearing your heart on torn sleeves
is that there's no place left to sew it

and so i have been looking for a home for this bleeding organ
since before i was a poet

taped to the knuckles of a closed fist
between the tight folds of screeching vocal cords
glued to the bottom of a wandering sole

i've found so many wrong answers
solutions that never worked for me

searching for a breast pocket
proudly on display
my one chance at feeling freed
my one chance to create my own healed space

i feel like everyone assumes it's equal opportunity
like we all start with the same shirt with intact sleeves

like we have a similar shot at letting ourselves be
but it seems

like i never learned how to do anything
but bleed
    scream
    dream of a day when i might find myself whole
    fixed and patched up
    sewn at the seams and glued up
    back into one piece

like i was ever in one piece to begin with

healing, but never healed

light these bones
let it be shown
illumine this skeleton
these fires deep within
highlight this shell i'm in
my boundaries, my jagged edge
show me as whole as i could dream to be
with scattered pieces waiting to be cast again

the bone throwers won't throw me no more
weathered calcium lumps
too worn to be read
i leave the readers stumped
and so likewise i am a source
of confusion and dread
maybe because i never learned
where i wanted my light to land

i am the toppled lantern
kerosene across the floor
so many would run
in fear from the flames
but truly in this dancing firelight
i could set my soul ablaze

and i fear i am the ever-healing contusion
the wounded piece so determined to mend
just never quite there
the sore that is constantly picked at
scabbed over only to be plucked raw again
maybe bleeding is the healthiest thing i can do

a real relief

i'm scared,
of all things
of pressing my fingers
too hard to the crease

of letting the ink imprint
a real impression of my brain

of folding my true heart
between the edges of the page

i'm scared you'll see
that i'm too far gone
and too broken to save

why would i write with self-restraint?

i feel like a heathen
every time i pick up the pen
as though i'll never belong
in this bright and beautiful world as real poets do

should i write of the splendor before me?
or of the gnashing teeth
and bloodstained hands behind me?

should i fill these pages with praises of the glories
real poets have brought to life and shared?
or should i clear the closet of the rotting corpses
i've left to wither too many winters?

maybe letting myself write down this darkness in me
soothes the beast inside we all struggle to keep at bay

so let me hate what i write
so let me write what i hate
at least i was brave enough to let me say it

needy

i am afraid
that ONLY for every INCH that i give
i am allowed to take

'cause
        some
                days
                        i need
                                feet

coping loud

she always likes to hear me sing

not like i do it that often

likes to hear me bare my soul, vibrate a tone
to contrast the bleakness i feel in my bones

not like i do it that often

she always likes to hear me sing
as though making my goodbyes more musical
might make them hurt less against this hole in my chest

and she always likes to hear me say
maybe tomorrow WILL hurt less,
bring fewer repetitions of pain
even though each new day has always seemed
to bring worse punishment than it's saved

and she likes to hear me sing

not like i do it that often

how many children have we lost?

i woke today in a
mostly
warm bed
i shivered a little
but there was a cup of tea
and a blanket for me
and that was enough

i worked today
got my hands dirty with fresh soil
dirt caked into fingernails
listened to a little music
and smiled to myself
maybe this would be okay

i made plans today
like tomorrow was actually promised
could be guaranteed
i thought
isn't this wonderful
all this love and pain
this life i hold
maybe i could share it someday

maybe someday i could be a father
have a family of my own
dreams that for a while
i never thought i would build a home around

i thought
i could love my family
show them some of the joys to be experienced
and hold them through the grief
of simply having lived long enough to endure loss

i could be a dad
wouldn't that be wild

and make my whole world
out of the souls who i watched grow
and let them go someday
when they've found their own way
maybe

oh how i would love to be a father
i thought

and in the news today i heard
the story of a father
who maybe one day not long ago
was just like me
full of hopes and life and love

i heard the story of a father
who found out today
after he survived the airstrike
that the burning remains of his whole world
could fit in pieces
into a single, crumpled, plastic bag

goodbye, Tyler, 'till we meet again

i caught myself
looking in the mirror
trying to explain some way

that my friend is in a place
where they need not worry
about fighting today

like it is some relief
or some touch of grace

like there isn't a hole in my heart
the size of the part
that you filled with laughter

yet for matters such as these
looking for comfort
leads me to examining
the new wrinkled line across my face

so i sit here with questions like
where have you gone?
and why now, of all days?
will it be me next
who leaves to follow you the same?

catharsis

smile at what life brings you
be thankful for the second chances given
cherish what is fleeting

you will scream when it leaves you
abandoned and bleeding
on a floor of broken dreams
and jagged memories

you will ache
as the lights leave your soul
and your heart tears itself into the pieces
you worked so hard to make whole

-

scream, little one
growth does not come without pain
do not be afraid
scream
crack the glasses
and shake your pieces   into   places
                        back   their

scream

seeking with ballpoints

i want to write,
write frenetically.

i am tired of existing
only to be present ephemerally.

it might be my challenge
for all of this eternity.

simply to find myself.

but for too many moments

        i have lost myself in the sensation of fighting.

    for too many moments

        i have lost myself in the sensation of running.

    for too many moments

        i have lost myself in the sensation

    for too many moments

        i have lost myself

        i have lost myself.

        haven't i?

grade school shame

you see
with my version of bipolar
my brand of anxiety
before i knew what was up
i heard a lot of the same
a lot of what brought me shame
a lot of what sounded like

shut up

3rd grade math
the others are trying to learn

shut up

4th grade science
you're a distraction
you're a nuisance

shut up

5th grade english
the others read in silence

shut up

6th grade science
go back to dissecting your frog

shut up

7th grade
by the second week of algebra
i was shoved into the back corner of the room
a table to myself
so that i didn't have anyone to talk to

i learned that year
to *shut up*
keep my head down
pretend i was a fly on the wall

nothing more than another silent head in the room
with no ideas, no creativity, no spark
just a pair of open ears to sponge up
what the teachers thought was important

shut up

8th grade band
those are supposed to be rests, not a chance to talk

shut up

9th grade english
smart aleck, know-it-all, pretentious to think you can speak yet

shut up

10th grade i started to hum
happy to make quiet sounds that felt authentic

afraid of hearing again

shut up

11th grade
i joined a choir
learned to sing with with my chest out
and thought it was all on the up-and-up from here
not a need to worry

12th grade

shut up

no one wants to hear from you
just be quiet
matter of fact
go fuck off

and *shut up*

-

how about this
i came to write
i came to speak
maybe this head of mine
has ideas that are big enough to scare you
pompous enough to annoy you

but i came to speak my truth

my tongue was not made to be bitten

to choke on these words
to swallow this music

i will not shut up

self-immolation (some warmth from me)

i must confess
i feel like a monster
with this sheepskin
dragging me
                down

yet in these rising tides
i have tied to my wrists
the limp bodies of all my traumas
as though i could ever swim to the top
AND
gloat as though i could be
somehow better than the past that made me

and i was not born with the strength
to carry the weight of other people's problems
but i will sit here
with you
in the darkness through them

but i must confess
i feel like a monster
it is these bones that burn me
the same ones you call "illuminating"

a fire from the inside
a death sentence of a reassurance
but i feel called
to help bring light to the shadows i see

and i must confess
i love you
so here, in these pages
i will burn for free

hickory nut mountain road

i started the ride with two jackets
one for the wind
one for the cold

then i saw
that light bar
in the middle of the road
with headlights
almost touching the ground

and if i hadn't been curious enough
to slow down and look
i would've hit him

laying on his side
red streaking down his face
ripped jacket and jeans
the yells

"where is my wife"
he asked me

i couldn't even see another body
and he wants me to leave him behind
to go look for her?

but he insisted
and with no other way to placate him
i left him with my jacket

another body
in the ditch this time
more blood

i can't tell if i'm seeing muscle or bone
at the moment i don't care to know
but heads shouldn't be bleeding that much

she's freezing but can respond
and i left her with my jacket

they are both difficult to make sense of
words slurred and unfocused
and as another rider arrives and tries to help
by hiding beer cans in the woods
the struggle for consciousness takes everything
when the only thing they can feel is the pain

9-1-1 says they're on the way, but it's been ten minutes
and shit i'm shivering but that's the best damn thing
i can come up with to do
when there's no medical care i know of to help

"just keep them awake" they said
so i listened to the cries
left my jackets to warm them and shivered

when we flagged down the first responders
volunteer firefighters handed me gloves and gauze
told me to apply pressure to her head

it needed to be done
but watching her face roiled in pain
nearly turned my stomach

twenty more minutes for the ambulance
i guess that's a long dirt road for you
and they finally arrive with the stretchers
i couldn't tell if the two were awake
until the paramedic
began moving the bodies
mostly limp except for the shouts of pain

i got my wind jacket back and overheard
two birds to fly
open fracture
possible hip

concussions
multiple lacerations
evac immediately

and as i watched them go
still in shock of the pain and the cold
staring at the mangled four wheeler
and asking too many questions
too many times

i hope the jacket keeps them warm

endure

see
here's my plight
i hate what i write
i hate to bring darkness to the light
to quiver and to shake each night

i bear this infection
cursing this blight

i wish for one second
that i could heal with these words
i wish for one second
for something benevolent that i could be heard

i just want to make this world glow
cast in flame
alight with the fire of my soul

but every time i write
i hate the words
the phrases
the meanings
the placements
it all feels despicable

and maybe this is a pity party
my stocking full of coal
maybe this is my shadow self
self-sabotaging the whole

maybe i'll never know

but i guess i'll keep writing
keep baring my soul
i'll keep showing up to life's well
with an empty bowl

i just know
one day the light will shine
and the future will not be so distant
and i can proudly call these writings mine
and know the darkness was just an instance
along a timeline sublime

begging for renewal

bring the rain
the thunder to shout down my shame
cleanse this parched, bone-dry brain
remind me of the feeling
of flowing freely like these drops upon my face

take the pain
i am but a moment from abluvion
at the precipice of being washed away
melancholy in my moments
that i might slip today

and when the storms come
may the waters renew me
finding strength and sure feet
to the sound of a new beat
help me to see another day

ruins

love me as one would a broken castle
ruined ramparts that welcome instead of block now
hollowed out by a great fire
a place where there is now room for something new to grow

love me as though you were to bear witness
to the terrible things that have happened here
unspeakable events that used to take place
yet now the old ways have been abandoned
cast aside
forgotten with time

know that you may never know
the extent of the tragedy
carried in this frame
but these bones still stand
these bones still hold space
a derelict, broken cage
now a shelter for new beginnings
that walk these old halls

and as i am reclaimed
love me as i fade
as determined as i once was
now to cradle life in my shade
and as i am worn down
let the elements take me
slowly

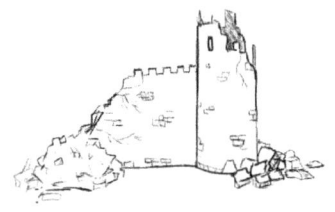

seaglass

i guess i never spoke up
never stood there and said it out loud
never let the words flow
from the back of my mind
to the front of my mouth

i love you

i hate you

i love you

i am afraid of you

i want you

to know that i wish there was something i could do
about this fucking head of mine

and isn't it ironic
like broken glass in the sand
how i'll wait here and stand
like the journey hasn't ground me down
made me into who i am

but maybe the rough edges will weather
jagged knives to gentle hugs

maybe with time
i'll slowly just come undone

anxiety

"for you," i say to me
song

so just keep on biding your time
stay lost in your mind
tryna see through
the fears
keeping you locked up inside

i know you really wanna open your heart
bare your soul and depart
from the fears
that no one's
ever gonna welcome your spark

so let's dance around the fire at dark
i'll speak flames from my heart
so you can too
'till the sun
brings us back around to the start

and so i'll keep on biding my time
staying lost in my mind
tryna see through
the fears
keeping me locked up inside

pace

and for a while i will just be
pacing the floorboards of an almost empty apartment
while the sun caresses the screen
a march that anyone who saw
would swear my skin leaks anxiety
but for me
it is a motion of relaxation
a chance to rest against my foundations
lose thought, lose fervor, lose temptation
a chance to be at peace
while my soles tread the same ten feet
sipping warming beer and postponing my time to eat
i am indecisive in this decision
maybe i'll do this
'till i find new dreams

kronos

blossoming thought
and my dream's sequence for naught
let me forget
every reason for which i fought,
be swept away with a belly of rocks

may i eat my past,
my children/my fears,
may i whisper away
the enemies i hold dear

flesh or gravel
may my tongue reminisce
recall things how i wish
rather than
to simply be pieces in an abyss

i'm too anxious to ever give a ted-talk

thank you for coming to my ted talk
sorry
that's just filler
for when i can't get off my soapbox

it's in these moments i realize
my words can't walk
and the sounds s
            p
          i
           l
           l
               from my throat
        like aftershocks
weighted

you see, i like to speak spoof
a touch out-of-touch with the truth
trying to imagine tomorrow
as a whole other room

it is a performance
to avoid the reality before us
or rather to imagine
that the darknesses abhor us

enough to vacate the sunrise
maybe leave us with dry eyes
and abandon their habits
of half-truths and blindsides

maybe tomorrow i'll be free
without hiding in the subtlety
at peace with who i see
maybe tomorrow i'll be me

step up to the mic, row

i'm trying to get used to this attention
this feeling of tension
electric under my skin
i'm convinced it's a lesson

i'm standing here to see
that this world is not out to get me
trying to recover a missing piece of my personality

you see, i used to feel bulletproof
the one who could take the room
shake the roof
speak my truth

i gave speeches literally
got a little change for talking figuratively
but recently it's been relatively upside down
and i guess that's just something
i'm still trying to wrap my head around
fear is a part of me
i'm not immune to impact, like hitting the ground

maybe it all finally caught up to me
the doc says it's anxiety
a tumor in the pituitary
manic-depressive and emotionally suppressed... it's

just one thing after another
regardless i'm here
trying to get used to this tension
getting comfortable with the attention
up the creek with no paddle
but learning my lesson
i'm still rowan

only one
song

said life got me feelin'
feelin' so small
wanna break from those moments
wanna escape from it all

so i came a knockin'
up to that ole' wooden door
said that i wouldn't knock it
'till i stepped to the floor

and i'll say

i'm only one
i'm only me
learning to love
just being free
ain't nothing else
i'd rather do
than waste this moment
right here with you

now it's here i come runnin'
into your open arms
and it's here i'll keep comin'
please don't do me no harm

i know sometimes i get scared
i hope you know that ain't me
it's just another head risin'
call it anxiety

learning to let down my guard here
learning to loosen my tongue
you know these words might just help me
learn to finally have fun

and i'll say

i'm only one
i'm only me
learning to love
just being free
ain't nothing else
i'd rather do
than waste this moment
right here with you

from this light i've been hidin'
and all the people who stare
finally learnin' my lesson
just be weird and don't care

now i call this the fool's dance
the way i'm shakin' my bones
is it fear or a tap dance
don't know if anyone knows

in this light i'll keep dancin'
on the tips of my toes
runnin' in circles
'til i find myself whole

and i'll say

i'm only one
i'm only me
learning to love
just being free

ain't nothing else
i'd rather do
than waste this moment
right here with you

so here's to the weirdness
and to you here my friends
may we find ourselves some peace
so we can laugh 'till the end

prayer/meditation

phoenix

i would argue
that writing rips the skin
turns ink to blood
in this exacerbating pen

i would argue
that writing bares the heart
three glorious seconds to bleed
before the flatline needs a spark

i would argue
that this writing will kill me
and all of my old versions
from which i wish to be apart

welcome to my funeral

writer's block

the perfection of space
the compromise the reality
and the beauty of thought

blank page after blank page
i am greeted by a full mind
with but a pencil
to brave the undisturbed

and i wish to gather
all of myselves
within a single of these moments

that i might entrust
my most elusive of hearts
amidst these pages

i didn't even pay a therapist to tell me this

hello.
i'm not quite sure what to say

you see, today
was supposed to be the day

when i looked at my shit, and got it sent
packed up
organized
in time to pay rent

but this time, like last time
i spent three hours in bed
avoiding responsibility
pretending it's all my authority
that i left the ideas [in my head]

too afraid to spit it out
write it down only to cross it out

maybe i'm just too scared
the room will laugh me out

-

little one

there are *millions* of rooms
and **billions** of souls

if you must, envision the goal
a room YOU built
packed and full
bursting with love
for the art of your soul

never give up the artist

listen little one

there is no art in your soul
art IS your soul

lay out the battles you've fought
the paths you've walked
the lessons you've been taught

what has stoked the flames of your heart
and filled your ribcage with thunder?
what has shown you your own power
to tear the world's seams asunder?

what has brought you
face to face with the whole
and braved the depths of bone
all to introduce to you your soul?

bear this art forward

keep creating

when tomorrow comes
song

just tell me when tomorrow comes
we'll be sipping on sunshine
've put down the swords
and picked up the red wine
tell me when the morning comes
tell me it'll be alright

yea i've been giving my all
for what feels like a lifetime
striving to thrive
with no rest and no down time
tell me will tomorrow come?
it's just another question of mine

see i've been trying so hard
to fit my head up my asshole
ignoring the signs
that we're headed for black holes
tell me if the morning comes
tell me we'll be alright

well if we are fighting
and i catch you crying
it's a win for me
cause me and mine ain't dying
at least that's what they've conditioned us to say
but isn't there a better way?

so tell me when tomorrow comes
we'll be sipping on sunshine
've put down the swords
and picked up the red wine
tell me when the morning comes
tell me it'll be alright

label me as you please

i spent the better part of the day thinking about labels
the way i've scribbled "table" on a post it note
and left it atop the furniture in the middle of the living room
the way i've scratched the word "frog"
next to the inanimate guardian above the fireplace
the way the name "Tim" sits next to a small pumpkin in the kitchen

i'm trying to understand what these mean
what expectations they bring
what labels make me a me?

the same way i'm trying to understand why i keep writing the word "rebel"
on the inside of my wrist
held close like a reminder to breathe that definition in
held close like a reminder to keep fighting for what i believe in

just how often do we label
just throw things into boxes that were never meant to be constrained
to be limited
how often have we lied to each other
and lived under a glass ceiling
that we've become so familiar with it might as well be made of cement

"how are you?"
"well, i'm... [good]"
"hi, who are you?"
"oh, i'm [rowan]"
"can i ask, are you a [man]?"

another label
another [box]
limiting myself, this human soul
to a couple of words trying to communicate the infinite

what labels make me a me?

i don't know

but i do know
i just want to live free
and die loving

whatever that makes me

patience
song

i'm seeing all of my old friends
with spouses and kids
thinking 'bout what was
but it is what it is

don't know what life's got
for me in its plans
just counting pennies and cups
what can fit in these hands

and i'll say

have patience on the path you are walking
there ain't another life to live
so keep laughing while you're talking
and there's grace in all these bridges you are building
have patience on the path you are walking

guessing which of these words
might just happen to stick
makes every time i step up
i swear i feel like i'm sick

i wish for once in my life
that my stomach would quit
but it's a hopeless wish
so i'll keep writing this

and i'll say to myself

have patience on the path you are walking
there ain't another life to live
so keep laughing while you're talking
and there's grace in all these bridges you are building
have patience on the path you are walking

you know i came here tonight
just to see how you are
love, for the moment
you're a bright shining star

wish i could give you the world
but i can give you my heart
peace on your path
i hope you love where you are

and remember

have patience on the path you are walking
there ain't another life to live
so keep laughing while you're talking
and there's grace in all these bridges you are building
have patience on the path you are walking

note to self: don't tear another ACL

give me the sunrise
after the lost rays
of wounded days
it seems sunbeams never hugged this face
with the tender promise
the gentle hug
saying "start fresh"
saying "rest a while"
saying "heal steady"
saying "the pain of yesterday can't reach you here"
"dry your eyes"
"stand up"
maybe being broken
letting the pieces of me crash
will give the artist of time enough material to work with
to craft something of me that might just last

Sir Edward Bulwer-Lytton would be mad at me for this

run from your loneliness little one
scream into the void just a bit louder
like maybe something, someone will call back
tell yourself
you already have all of the answers
you've learned the lessons
fought the fights
ran the races

pretend you can just CREATE
something better for yourself with nothing but the thought
with nothing except imagination
keep telling yourself it doesn't take work
keep lying, saying the pieces will fall into place

the pen is mighty
but it is time to grab the sword

facing

if you live your life believing
you will only feel death
on the day you pass from this earth
you will spend your life running

trading minutes for moments
and seconds for heartbeats
to make life mean something
before death steals your soul
and all becomes nothing

but what is life without death?
does one not define the other?
aren't they two sides of the same coin?
utterly inseparable
one begins
only for the other to follow
and then another beginning has arrived
so then what else are we alive to face?
and why else are we alive
but for us to face this cycle?

you see, i believe we die
in every day and in every moment
shedding old versions, old lives
be it in our bodies or in our minds
suffering will come to us all

and it is YOUR choice
if you wish to run
until your clock expires
but death will still come

i believe that life is.
in spite of death

life is.

life continues.
life endures.
life rises *through* the ashes of death

when death stings at your flesh
to pull the flames from your chest
life is to stand tall and say
that you will not succumb today

and when death stares through us in the mirror
pulling its dark curtains over the mind
life persists through the pain
leaking from the corners of your eyes

when death calls your name
i believe life is to say
that you are done running
and will not live in flight today

when tomorrow arrives
will you choose to live
or to die afraid?

plunge

i wished this would lift me up
past the broken knuckles
and this emaciated figure

i wished it would help me to soar
that these pages could be folded
into feathers upon feathers
paperweight wings
to carry a weary sore soul

for a moment i wished
i could drop my own weight
float out into the blue
a sky as light as my dreams

but like the wave that rises, that lifts
i must first
                    sink, must be dragged
                                        down to the
                                                depths
like the arrow which whistles forth
imustbepulledbackwardsfirst

so i will look to the sky
standing, toes gripping the edge
write of my dreams to fly

and i will f
            a
            l
            l
            .
            .
            .

how the birds must dream/clarity of a written heart

to soar like the eagle's wings might carry you
to fly and to rise
to dip wings in the basins of clouds
to   and to d
    drop   i
                v
                 e
to fold 'neath the skies
to careen across the mountain heights
to swoop, a figure alight
plummeting miles only to stretch and to glide
to see the lows with clarity from the highest of highs
to know that this world lies
for a moment
beneath you
just as equally as it is responsible for your privilege of flight

subjective soothing

they say
music will soothe the savage beast

and i agree

one thousand percent of the time
in every situation

under one stipulation

define "music"

life - to experience, not to solve

answers
answers
to life
to the universe

everyone wonders
why are we here
what are we living for
is there more in store

they look for
answers
asking each other
asking god
asking the stillness
after hearing your parents breathe their last
asking the cries
in the pale morning of a maternity ward
asking the reflection
that never looked this old before

what's next
what are we fighting for

why does the sun come up
only to show us the same light as yesterday
why do the tides ebb
only to crash against the shore
with the very same water
that was receding a moment before

maybe answers
were never what we were searching for

reminder/prayer

we are a source of energy
we are our own torch in the night
we sustain our life through the earth
we sustain our life for the earth

we exchange our energy
with the life around us

breathe in

we work to keep our energy positive
and it is from sunlight we receive
our most important of blessings

breathe out

let tension and negativity go
and with the moonlight
ease my emotions to flow

always be thankful for good energy
and seek to repay it charitably

be patient with negativity
intercede if necessary
listen for advice, knowledge
and heed to greater empathy

guidance/affirmation

as above, so below
to my highest self
i release control

as without, so within
be love, my eternal mantra
my constant hymn

as the universe, so the soul
may my energy seek
the frequency of all

may my self become
a true representation of my soul

to manifest this affirmation
may lifelong growth be my goal

continue

breathe peace into the wings of the world
lay gently your touch upon all souls

for positivity, respond with reciprocity
negativity, allow peace to take hold

bear to the forefront of the mind
the heart values being
not good
not evil

those are but judgements of the self
and life values being

without words or language
existence continues

without labels or constraints
life continues

let not the mind nor the body
limit the possibility
of truly embracing existence
in whatever form it may choose

tbh i have no idea what kundalini really is

awaken the serpent
enter the world
embrace the moment
of becoming whole

fine-tune the senses
let love fill the soul
breathe peace upon these bones
and bring purpose to these goals

crying for finches beneath the windowsill

i swear i'm still looking for something
just the little something that will fix me
this puzzle frames a beautiful portrait
but the piece missing is the twinkle of life in my eye
it's not even like this life is terrible, horrible
some amalgamation of awful
it's just that it's never felt quite right
quite at peace

as beautiful as it is to hold the life of a small bird in your palm
yet as terrible as it is to watch the gorgeous finch slowly fade
its broken wings unmendable
despite your hopes, powers, dreams

this life rests in my hands
mine to shape
mine to change
mine to embrace
but how to give it meaning
how do i give it purpose and grace
how do i cultivate in this life the feeling
that none of these tears will go to waste

caution: beating heart

be careful with me
not because these bones are brittle
but because they store every trauma
i claim has ever hurt me, even a little

be careful with me
not because this head is frightful, fleeting
but because of its steady, patient reading
there is so much that will never be said

be careful with me
not because this heart is weak
but because it beats a wild forest song
every day, every night, every dusk so bleak

be careful with me
it is not because i lack strength
but because for far too long
i have tried and been taught to carry on
with an empty vessel and a work song
i have been encouraged
from the start of my time
to yank at every f-i-b-e-r of these bootstraps
'till i am at peace with what i call mine

my life
my happiness
my heart
my mind

my friends
my love
my spark
my time

be careful with me
i beg you

be careful with me
lest i add you to the list
of what i encircle in these arms

be careful with me
lest i put you to the test
of being worth enfolding
into the pages of my heart

change comes
song

come some day
when i've a different name
different sins
and a different game

i'll take on faith
that i'll find my way
i changed from yesterday
i can change today

but please raise your hand
if you've ever said
don't worry 'bout me
when your heart is lead

look all i know
is we'll be okay
we're just learning to love
and fighting to stay

so when change comes
for the depths of your soul
keep your arms wide open
and your spirit gold

full of holes
song

i know my demons ain't cold
i know my heart's full of holes
but i know that wherever i go
you'll be here

i know i've abandoned myself
pretended to be somebody else
but i know at the end of the day
you help me wash that away

see i spent
too long in the mirror this morning
ignoring what my heartbeat keeps calling
for me to live free in my own skin
take pride and go all in
see i've been living two lives at the same time
a foot in the world a foot in my mind
yeah i've been walking this tight line
with these two faces i call mine

i know my demons ain't cold
i know my heart's full of holes
but i know that wherever i go
you'll be here

i know i've abandoned myself
pretended to be somebody else
but i know at the end of the day
you help me wash that away

here's to
you and everyone in this room
you get me through my blues
when you choose
to see me in the same light as you

and when i'm on my knees in the evening
you pick me up you find me breathing
so i give this song up to you
and choose to be grateful

'cause i know my demons ain't cold
i know my heart's full of holes
but i know that wherever i go
you'll be here

i know i've abandoned myself
pretended to be somebody else
but i know at the end of the day
you help me wash that away

so when you
fall down and you feel like calling
for help but you don't know who's waiting
and when you're at the end of your line
just call mine i'll be on time
and when you're staring at the mirror and it's broken
your heart's beating too fast and you're hoping
for a better tomorrow
i hope you know

that i know your demons ain't cold
i know your heart's full of holes
but just know that wherever you go
i'll be here

i know you've abandoned yourself
pretended to be somebody else
just know at the end of the day
that's okay

yea i know your demons ain't cold
i know your heart's full of holes
but just know that wherever you go
i'll be here

phoeniX

i would argue
that writing cleans the soul
flakes away the decay
and reflourishes the whole

i would argue
that writing restores the veins
like a bypass and a stent
it relieves the shame

i would argue
that this writing will recreate me
in the image of a self
with hands held open
as soft and delicate as grace

welcome to my birth

hope

wellspring

i wish to write deeply
not speak sheepishly
with both hands in the well
of this life
which especially loves those of us
who bears its charge earnestly

cupping more water
i'm trying

i wish to take myself seriously
this muse, this inner deity
may i honor her
and cherish her proclivities

cupping more water
may i be giving my all freely

i wish that this life not catch me
in my throes of acting sleepily
dare i to have both eyes open
my spirit taking charge of this synergy

when i wake in the morning
let the dawn find the most of me

cupping more water
i'm here
making the most of me
trying
making the most of me

i guess i'll learn to lay (my own) bricks

i think that i have believed almost my whole life
that if i want to be accepted
all i need
is to trust the process
is to follow the path
is to keep my head down
and do the 'right' thing

i'm getting to the point now
where there is no more path ahead of me
no one is left to lay the yellow bricks
no one remains to chart my course through the darkness
that job is up to me
and with it the certainty
some will be displeased
hate me
be loveless towards me
consider me unwise

but i must become my own fighter
my own advocate
and my own lighter

so if i want to be accepted
i'm sure there's someone out there
if i want to be loved
i'm sure i will find a soul who cares
if this is what i want
then i will never pretend to be someone else to find it
never fr a gm en t myself
never show myself as pieces of an incomplete whole
i will never show anything less than my authentic soul

teach me

today i looked in the mirror
and fearfully recognized moments of apathy
then i thought about what the trees do
underground
inches, no, feet, no, yards beneath the topsoil
that reaching, branching, clambering for connection
that hand of comfort in the deep dark beneath loam
that "i will feed you when you're hungry and give water when you thirst"
all because "i know you'd do the same for me"
maybe the dark truth of the forest
is simply the depth by which the thing itself
cares, craves, yearns to help
                    to save
                    to nurture
maybe the dark shadow of the trees
could be the bright spark in my heart

better versions

what if tomorrow came today?
showed up to the door in the pouring rain
knock knock knock
let her in
don't you know it'd be rude to make her wait
to make her ask again
what if the 'you' that you showed up as today
inspired a change
paved the way
wrote a new chapter
for all who watched to read
who would that 'you' be?

my version of me
would sit with a little less shame
would take care to point fewer fingers in blame
would hold peace and love in every cell of this brain
i would show the world
a reason to remember my name

with ink in these veins
heart pumping like an old freight train
if you'd cut me i'd bleed
but oh, would i paint
across the canvas of life
every dream in this frame
i would paint
a thousand peaceful still-lifes
for every fear i've felt that's stayed
and i would write
with this pitch-black blood on a world so bright

they say contrast adds definition
adds appreciation
like you'd never be grateful for a day
if the night wasn't so eager to snatch the time away

and i would write
of the darkness and the fight
of all the times i held my own frame
curled and rocking through the night
i would show the world every low i've stumbled through
if for no other reason
than to show when it gets worse
there's still a reason to keep the fight too

maybe that's the 'me' i'd be
maybe i'm still learning to see
what person will stand in these shoes
when the future comes and tells
that there is everything to lose

what you will you be?

depth (probably forced)

i just wish i could convince you i'm thinking
that deep behind these eyes there is some feeling
some thought
some passion
something quite so profoundly revealing
i wish i could show you the flurry
that my restless synapses carry
the anxious dance
of always wanting to say the right thing
of always wanting to show i have something of meaning to say
maybe i might never be realized
fully seen and recognized
as a free thinking me
but dare i to hope to never stop trying
never give up the brush and let the paint dry
dare i to never let go of this chance
to bridge my world and yours
and show there is a life in this heart

committal of (old) faith

i was born a soul
i was raised to be a christian
yet i haven't called myself such in years
i'm sure many wonder if my faith is still a part of me
i'm sure many wonder if i am still the person
i was raised to be

how could i be?

i've seen so many christians dying on the crosses
they've built with their own two hands
and convinced themselves that to die was what god meant for them

i've seen so many of my former kin stuck in their hearts and minds afraid
thinking that this world is lost
filled with the godless and faithless
who 'tear this world at its seams'

but i believe that we were not born to die

i believe we all hold the divine in our hearts
and the future in our minds

i believe i am like any other
one whom christians would probably call
'faithless,' 'broken,' 'lost,' and 'wandering'

but i wear my heart on my sleeve
and hold my faith in my chest
because where else could they be kept?

i hold my truth in my throat with the gentleness of eggshells
because what makes me free is unique to me

i share my love with the souls i meet
because it is in giving i know that i pursue
the quickest route to set myself free

i have learned that understanding comes at the cost
of letting my soul be seen

i have learned that to be known as the being my god made me
requires nothing less than absolute courage and bravery

i am determined to live
hopefully just as the divine intended for me
faithful and perseverant
discovering the path the universe has laid out before me

i have forgotten the lessons of the bible
but i have found words here in my community
that teach peace to my mind and breathe life into my spirit

i have forgotten the words of jesus
but remembered that it is with love we can save

i used to call myself christian
but i chose to leave behind words
that align me with the people
who believe it is god's will to fear and to hate

i have faith
that tomorrow will be waiting eagerly for us
when we drop the phobias and stand up to the hate
when we seek understanding from each other instead of retribution or pain
when we offer our lives to being guided by love instead of fear and shame

i have faith
that maybe i can help be a part of that change

thank you macklemore

one of my favorite songs
plays this reminder as a balm

*"if you preach hate at the service
those words aren't anointed*

*and that holy water
that you soak in has been poisoned"*

i guess hearing it helps keep me sane
because i know too many voices that **scream** blame

i know too many echoes
of anger and shame

people who are so scared of the unfamiliar, the unknown
they would claim righteousness with a hateful tone

i hope out of all the messages i hear
and all of these words i write and hold dear

that i'll never bring hate to the page
that my words will be founded on love uncaged

i hope that when it's tomorrow's age
there will be peace with no room for this hateful haze

lead by example, lead by dreams

for once in my life it feels like i'm dreaming
actively reaching
with both hands seeking
a better tomorrow for myself
where i find joy and wealth
not money and hollow satisfaction

i feel as though i have a whole universe of possibility
in the other side of the mirror staring back at me
daring me to take the leap
take a chance
saying if you don't play for keeps
it'll never last

what do i want this legacy to be?
someone who played it safe?
took the easy path?
or someone who risked everything
to find their true self
the version that will outlast
stand the test of time
the halls of memory
and hold stories i can pass to mine
i think want to leave behind
a story my children can follow
one that leads to happiness and peace
with no return date labeled 'tomorrow'

fade

i am determined
to never let anyone else
carry the weight of my shadow for me

it is attached to me for a reason
let me be
to wallow and to ache
to strive and to shake
to earn the light
that will illumine this darkness to fade

to become a spouse

my dear
for you i would run the ramparts
rampant with my heart

might i give myself
the chance to be seen
not for money, but for wealth
hidden in these dreams

-

to become a father

oh to be at peace with the heart
without a conflagration to start
except for the beating
at the beginning of one's own part

-

to become a grandfather/to say goodbye

oh my love
when it is time you will fly
and the breadth of your soul
might embrace the sky

oh my love
when it is time you will fly
That, i hope i might live to see
past my body's time

affirmation and expectation

i will become what i deserve

i loved that affirmation
because i thought comfortably
if i kept my head down
my hands busy
and my feet moving in a good direction
everything would turn out alright

i will become what i deserve

i thought as though the universe would size me up
d
  r
   o
    p
     me where it wanted me to be
and let me rest easily

as though it could be so simple

in world like this that balances comfort with pain
the way i might casually
balance a pencil across my fingers

and i thought as though i wasn't a piece
of that very universe
deciding what i am deserving of

i will become what i deserve

am i not deserving   am i not deserving

of happiness?   of pain?
of joy?   of grief?
of light?   of loss?
of laughter?   of weeping?

what do i deserve?
in this weak, fallible self?
if i confine myself to be deserving of what i 'earn'
when will it ever be enough?
if i confine myself to be deserving of what i 'wish'
when will i ever stop wishing

see i think i've sat in the darkness
with other people's demons
for so long i can't recognize my own
as being any different from my friends
all this wishing, this wanting, this hurting

i've looked in this cracked mirror too many times
maybe i'm the only one who sees clearly
maybe i'm the only one who sees
how broken this reflection truly is

i will become what i deserve

i may never have an answer
to the question of deserve
but until i do
i will perseverate
   pushing forward
rowan along
until this universe is tired of me
walking around like i'm supposed to be here

i'll be the dandelions that break the concrete
the tree so thirsty it crushes your water pipes to drink
the rose's thorns to anyone who would dare
to cut the beautiful flowers without honoring
the effort it took to grow them

in this garden i'll keep growing
i take up s p a c e
i step on toes

even as i grow down dark streets
i still grow
clawing for the light
my space
my right
my chance to heal (to be alright)
and my chance to heal this world
as it is healing me

i will become what this universe asks of me

hospital discharge at twenty three

here's what i learned from my twenty three years
what i've fought for and yearned for while battling fears
everyone tried to tell me to turn to   god
yet it seemed   god   had nothing to learn

"if you're the smartest person in the room,
you're in the wrong room"

so get the fuck out of my house   god
here's what i learned from twenty three years
it's to spite   god   and all the damned fears
teach him there's at least one thing missing
from the hollowness between his ears

i pictured   god   as 'everyone else'

and   god   put me in the ring at three and a half years
said fight
hit back
and when i said no,
went as far as to kick me in the back

so i fought
fuck you   god,   i'm determined

god   broke my wrist, put me back on the edge of the ring
and said don't you run, you've gotta fight back

i lost, but when my second chance came
i had no time to wrap my hand
no strength to make fists
he still said fight
so i kicked his teeth in
twenty twelve youth grand champ
it was mine before i walked in
fuck you   god,   i'm determined

when i earned my second degree black belt
god   tied it around my eight year old hips
said i couldn't test again for a decade
"that's how it had to be" spilled from his lips
and god   said congrats
but his eyes said
boy, you'll quit before you can dream
so at eighteen and a half
i made god   tie that third degree around my damn waist
and i looked at him
fire in the eyes
fuck you god, i'm determined

at twenty one god   stepped with both feet in the cage
locked the door and spit in my face
put his fingers in my brain
filled my head with disorders, diseases, and shames
tempted me to fight
begged me to swing
i said god
you need to learn
you are not my enemy today
i asked for help
determined that god   would not remind me
of how fighting felt

i broke my hand all the same
i was determined to escape
and i did
through pain
through shame
putting blame
on anyone else
on anything else
but it wasn't you god
it was me
let me fix these veins
these hands
this brain

fuck you god, i'm learning too
i guess that's what you wanted me to do
i picked a new enemy today

fuck you god, i'm yearning
i'll be a better me
to spite what you say
you seem adamant to make me a fighter
so i'll fight to remake this soul
into the best thing i've been given in this world

this year, god put me in that hospital bed again
worn out and tired
and begging for another chance
i said god
why would you do this, break me down again and again?
why would you put me through this?

this time as i waited for him to swing
tired arms at my sides
i heard a small voice at the back of my brain
god said
"i thought you were determined"

so here's another take
another fight, and another chance to shake
the apple tree from which you fell
learning to fly again to escape your hell
what have you learned
from all this fighting
from all this war

god looked at me
and picked his hands up once more

and this time i think i got it
he was always the one i fought with
because that's what he does
back when i didn't know what i wanted

so when he swung this time
i didn't hit back
i put my hands out wide
and gave him a hug back

i said
fuck you   god
there's more to this moment
than the battles with which you taught me
there's love and there's hope
there's forgiveness for the broken

i said
fuck you   god
i'll love you till your hands are just as shattered
as the heart you're holding
trying to keep from being opened
so keep swinging
we'll see who laughs last
who's more determined in life
in these moments to stand fast
i AM determined
you made a warrior of me
now watch as i fight
to give love as easily as i breathe

to hope

my mother tells me
it's good to write
about the important things

so i tried
i tried

to write about the sky
the stars
the ocean
my heart

the high
the music
the forest
the art

how it feels
to laugh
to crash
to wish for one last

but i always seem to end up
just writing about you

the weight of hope

i keep asking myself the dangerous question
what am i worth?
its lethality sitting not at the point of a blade
but in the reflection of a mirror
what am i worth?

how do you ask such a question
without comparison robbing you of the joys of you?
dragging you down
under the heavy fist of criticality
a pallet of bricks we call "feelings of inadequacy"
what AM i worth?
and what is the weight of a soul?

many people start
with a look back
measuring what the past holds
so i guess to measure me
i could paint a picture from my beginning
to what my present has let unfold

i was
the hyperactive kid
always told
sit down, shut up
enthusiasm is gold
especially when it is too heavy to sit
on everyone else's shoulders

i was
the gifted and talented
know-it-all, one of the smartest in the room
usually because my head was too big
to fit anyone else new

i was
the bookworm
lost in every world except this one

i was
the youth national champion
two times gold
a fighting soul not even broken wrists could break
someone who fought with the thought
that violence would make
a world i'd actually be proud of living in

i was
the bullied and the bully
trauma leaking from bruised knuckles
like you actually deserved
the hatred i held for myself
like anyone did

i was
a promise of forever
extinguished before my lips
could finish the phrase

i was
the "text me back" kid
because i understood your sorrow
i understood you were in pain
please don't walk to the bridge
with no plans of walking back again

and i was
the one in pain
on the other end of the line
planning to tie myself a rope
a guideline
to tether me from then
into the next life

i was
the alcoholic
one drink away from forgetting the pain
the same drink away
from forgetting my own name

i was
the addict
chasing a high instead of a life
that might could actually mean something
by the time i settled my strife

i was
the shattered psychotic
both high and low
lucid and lost
free and shackled
with no sense of now, no sense of how
i could ever mend this soul
or how i could grow
beyond the broken pieces
that defined the w(hole)

you see, my past paints its picture
not gilded
not gold

but cracked pavement
with weeds in the road
but isn't the beauty
in the fact that life continues to grow?

i am not defined by the edges of the pavement
i am defined by my desire to show
that i will continue
at times growing slow
i will shatter the concrete
not bound by the sediments
only limited by my soul

to define myself from such a past
is more than just a box
it is a shackle, manacles to imprison
the possibilities of how tomorrow could unfold

i will learn from who i was
but i will not let it write today's story
nor change the hopes i hold

so i ask again
what am i worth?
so i ask again
what is the weight of my soul?

my soul is not worth its weight in gold
not worth its weight in diamonds
not even worth its weight in blood

my soul is worth its weight in soul
incomparable
never sell that shit short

i am the culmination
of my mother's hopes
my father's dreams
i am my brother's shield and seams
i am my grandmother's love
my grandfather's pride

i am these words of my heart
i am these actions of my spirit

and most importantly i am this growth
or at least i try to be

this thing we call hope
promises of a better tomorrow
or at least i try to be

that is what i am worth
hope
that is what you are worth too

bare

and i will make them see me
every raw piece of broken beautiful
every inch of scarred heart in this beating chest

i will make them witness
this war
this crusade
this battle
to clear the darkness from my own soul
i will show my   separate   parts   whole
as pure as they were made
in an image divine

a human
being
trying
living
to be better
     greater
     loving
      healing

with every fiber that makes me complete

may love radiate through my existence

love

little more

the sun doesn't light up the world
because people see it
the sun lights up the world
because it is <u>there</u>
at every sunrise
every noon
and every sunset

your art doesn't change the world
just because people see it
your art changes the world
because it is a part
of what it means to be human
and what it means to love

and goodness knows, today
we could definitely use a little more human
and a little more love

i'm a poet, of course i wrote one about you

to my guide in the night
i would ask
what is the source of your light?

science would say it is a reflection of the sun
but i don't think that's quite right

what gives you, the moon,
permission to shine so bright
to permeate my sight

i would ask
please
teach me your lessons
let me learn to fight
just as you do
to ever grace the heaven's nights

teach me of your presence
teach me of your patience
teach me of soft rays
that illumine a sky so spacious

teach me of your |ph|as|es|
ever changing
teach me of the night's spaces
teach me to cradle the gentle hope
of a world that wishes upon your graces

what do you whisper to the stars?

ouranos
mighty heavens

with your constitution
compiled of the cosmic kaleidoscope

who lays your stage out before me
and bares your sacred stories

to be retold in awe of your splendor

let your stars draw their tales
across the open pages of my heart
and let my soul be rewritten
in the image of the infinite

raw, it's better to stay that way

often i am caught
by the intensity of the world
the sheer breadth of beauty and wonder
and often i am caught
by the terrible tragedy
that not even a single of these glorious moments
could ever truly be captured
i could not hold this moment in my palm
regard it
share it
behold it
it must linger, its essence nestling
in the resting places of our minds
still all the beauty of this moment eventually escapes us

maybe at our best
we can hold these moments fondly for a while
maybe at our best
we can observe as these moments pass
maybe at our best
we can take in the whole experience as it presents itself
and maybe at our best
we can be that intense beauty
overwhelming and magnificent

"maybe at our best"
but i don't even think we need our best
like these moments
you simply are
beautiful
intensely so

umbral heart

this love i hold for you
knows nothing of fresh air
knows nothing of steady earth
knows nothing of sun's rays

this love i hold for you
does not choke as the oxygen burns
does not shake as the ground crumbles beneath our feet

blot out the sun
and in its shadow my heart will dance
like flames set free

this love i hold for you
comes free and rich and fierce
this love i hold for you
comes from the expense
of trading every wild fantasy and dream
for the perfection waiting in front of me

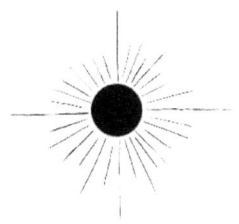

this poem is not about mud

i could tell you i missed the flowers
i could tell you i missed the soft sun,
slight breeze, vibrant greens
i could tell you i missed every high that's graced us
but the truth is i miss the mud
i miss the mud
the sticky, the swampy, the sticks-to-everything-imaginable
i miss the mud
the storms
the rains
i miss the aches and pains
the "work sucked" days
give me a thousand more "i hate this part of me"s
just for another chance to say
"i would choose you,
mud and all,
with every part of me"
i missed the mud
not because it's cozy and quaint
mainly because it lets me sit
right next to my favorite people
and together can't we weather
an awful lot of mud?

raison d'etre

i want people to know my why
the reason i came

quite frankly
i don't give a shit
if they remember my name

can't recall a word of my pain
block out and black out all of my shame

i want them to know my why
for these hands
for this head
for this heart
for this life
i want them to know
the reasons i came

a thousand words
will never contain
the multitudes of my heart
my soul
this infinite whole
being
i want the world to know
i want the world to grow
i want to water the roots
so they bloom wild and new
i want to fertilize the flower beds
drop nutrients on every damn seed

i want this garden to flourish
from the grass to the trees
whatever form you take
i hope you know this message is still meant for you
i want to reach out
these little gardeners hands

and watch you grow
encourage you grow
hope you grow
heal you grow
love you grow

i want you to know
that with every fiber in this heart
i think you're glorious
and now is the perfect time to start
to grow

lost in translation

i've been thinking lately
how to some, words have become
just this collection of l e t t e r s on a page
by who's splendid idea was that made?

they used to be more
symbols, hieroglyphs
before
they used to just be syllables
a sonic **roar**
a shout to the abyss
a feeble attempt to express duress
words used to be magic
a way to try to communicate
what we were [inside]

a way to fall short
of telling others
"i'm trying this time"
"i'm lying this time"
"help me, i'm crying inside"
"please god i feel alone this time"

its all a metaphor
trying to link brain wave to brain wave
but let me tell you
to us it could be so much more

so please bring up your metaphors
your poems
your songs
bring the words you held on to
just a little too long

i'll say it here
and no matter how clear
let me tell you
the words don't come near

to you whom i hold dear

i cherish you
i believe in you
and may you smile when you hear
i love you

meaning?

"stop"
"halt"
"brake"
"quit"
"pause"
"cease"
"desist"

clearly the words can change
while the meaning stays
consistent _____
         underneath

"how are you today?"
"you matter"
"have you eaten yet?"
"would you like a cup of tea?"
"you're inspiring"
"thank you for hearing these words"

_____

i love you

i hope you know
song

and i'd spend every second just searching
for an answer to why i need you
maybe 'tween all of these battles were fighting
there's no home i'd rather run to

with you here beside me i'm free now
to wash away the dirt off my soul
so here's one for today, we'll make it some way
and we're just praying to stay sticking around

so call me
when you get home
promise me you took it slow
and i hope you know
i just wanna see you grow
maybe laugh about it when we're old

so please keep using your heart for the healing
mending every piece of your soul
and when tomorrow comes calling i'll see you
in a light where we could stand on our own

and maybe all of this passion has meaning
every feeling a sign
yea it is what it is, but how it exists
is exactly what heaven looks like

so call me
when you get home
promise me you took it slow
and i hope you know
i just wanna see you grow
maybe laugh about it when we're old

existence outside of self-doubt

we deserve the freedom
the chance
to live again

to take broken wings
spread them wide
and fly again

we deserve the chance
to stand in our power
live by our truth
and speak the flames again

demand to honor yourself
in thought, word, and deed

take the time
the space
to listen for your needs

speak loud enough
for the people in the back to clap

take up so much space
so that it is useless to live in the past

you deserve to live free
not second guessing
if everything you've dreamed
will last

june - celebration

blue
think about it
picture the color

now realize that the shade in your head
is likely slightly different
from the shade in every other head in this world

i believe every word has a similar effect
a similar variation
let's try a different word

god

oooh that is not a pretty picture
in quite a few heads
especially for those of us who celebrate pride
especially for those of us
who have had the weapon of faith turned against them

let me clarify of which god i speak
because all too often
my friends told me of their god
a god they feared
a god they ran from
a god from whom they hid in shame
because too many had told my friends
they were not worthy of being god's creation
or of being loved

a god of wrath
a god of anger
a god of judgement
a god who would ask us
to hold hatred in our hearts
for the perfection of their own creation,
their own children

i refuse that god
i refute that god
i deny giving any credence or power to such a god
utterly

i was taught of a different god
to call them "the man in the sky"
and claim to know Their wishes
would be to put the infinite
into a box

i was taught of a different god
a god of multitudes
a god beyond our human conception of sexuality
a god beyond our human conception of gender
a god of mercy
a god of love
a god of compassion

a god that gave us a rainbow
so that all who saw it
would know that they are safe
and that they are loved

is that not the same safety and love
that we try to offer the youth?
and is it not wonderful that we use all of the colors
to celebrate all of the people,
to remind them that they belong
regardless of your queerness
regardless of your gender
especially because of those
even if you struggle to believe it yourself
we celebrate pride because
you are exactly who you are supposed to be
yourself

let's go back to this god
that i think made us all perfectly unique
i've heard of god the father
i've heard of god the son
but what about god the mother?
what about god the daughter?
god the sister?
god the brother?
god the friend?
god the lover?
what about god the compassionate stranger?
what about god the self?
didn't They give each and every one of us
a divine spark of perfection in our souls?
my faith would tell me yes

i think god does not beg for your hatred
there is already plenty enough of that
i think god begs for your love and your mercy

my faith would tell me that in loving yourself,
in accepting yourself,
and in turn by loving and accepting others
you acknowledge this divinity, this limitlessness, this perfection

coincidentally love and acceptance
define our month of celebration,
as we support and hold one another in this time

coincidentally pride is about loving ourselves
and loving our neighbors
exactly as we are

maybe
it's a coincidence that those messages
seem to overlap a little

maybe

happy pride

not every piece of you needs to change

a part of me will always breathe a sigh of relief, i think
when i realize i am not the person i used to be
i think that in some way i am always seeking an escape
a break from the person who made all of those mistakes
broke down
fucked up
who haunts every grave i've erased
a part of me wants to move on
acknowledging only the cracks that used to line my face

but maybe part of me
was the kind of person who could smile through the pain
laugh indiscriminately and at least try to light a way
maybe i'm scared to admit
that part of me was perfect enough to stay

ramble

with this writing
just who am i trying to save
and what cross am i bearing
onward to my grave
what message is my charge
do i think i have anything of value to say

p
r
o
b
a
b
l
y

n
o
t   lol

but i have spent all this time
to write, to write, and to write
i have gathered the whole of myself
to quit running and to fight
yet are these pages an escape?
a lock? or a key?
maybe an answer to life's plight
yet somehow always incompl...

well, let me take a swing
a wild shot in the dark
trying to synthesize a message
and cradle the flames
these brief sparks

what do you need to hear?
what do i need to hear?

maybe poetry is not enough to capture it
i wonder if the words even exist
to pull some universal truth
some secret to life's bliss

so what would i say
knowing the message is never complete
knowing this cup i carry is cracked
knowing what lies ahead of you is a longer dirt track

i guess i would say
know yourself
your heart
your soul
learn to hold a space for yourself
and cultivate love for this unimaginable whole

you are the infinite
in a world just as vast
whether you seek the truth externally or internally
it is your mission 'till you breathe your last

so no rush to get there

have patience and persistence
they will take you further forwards
and love yourself in this existence

for all we know
it is all we have

between the lines

someone told me the other day
you aren't really that straight
and you aren't really that gay

i told them you aren't really that wrong
i was made this way
turns out most people are like that anyhow
not a hundred percent hetero
not a hundred percent same

turns out most people
live at least a little in the in-between
and i'm just trying to get comfortable being me
trying to stop lying
that this soul is anything but heavenly
turns out i'm just trying to be honest
with the kind of person
i was made to be

loving.

thank you <3

babble

thank you for finding this page

the truth of the matter
is i have a lot to say
about nothing at all

and i can do nothing but pray
when my emotions feel

      small

so take these ramblings
with a grain of salt
and please enjoy today
as though it were your own damn fault

acknowledgements

thank you to my family, for every rough draft and rough tear you've held me through

thank you to my family at Wendesday Night Poetry, whose love and support has encouraged me to come home to you and myself

thank you to Kai and Doc, your open warm hearts have guided me and taught me more about what it means to live in poetry

thank you to Karen, for your constant supportive and insightful feedback and for your guidance while putting this collection together

thank you to Connor, for sharing your art and this vision with me

thank you, reader, for opening your heart to these words and sharing for a moment a glimpse into a version of myself that is still emerging

author bio

rowan stuart lay (he/they/+others) is an Arkansas native and poet who started writing poetry at age eighteen. Now after six years of writing and learning (from the start day of this book in June 2024), he has come to use writing as a way to express their heart and challenge himself to grow. rowan has spent time as a bookworm, a martial artist, a singer, a dancer, an advocate, a scholar, and a writer.

They hope that as more of life unfolds he can continue to look for the blessings and challenges to capture and turn into art that helps the world heal, feel seen, and grow into a healthier, more loving society (or at least a healthier and more loving self).

www.ingramcontent.com/pod-product-compliance
Lightning Source LLC
Chambersburg PA
CBHW051320120626
46547CB00015B/2317